Young Musician

Playing the

Flute

Recorder

and other

Woodwind

Simon Walton

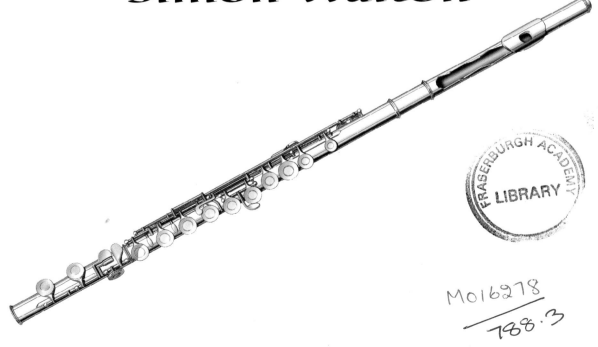

Franklin Watts
London • Sydney

INTRODUCTION

The flute family is one of the world's oldest groups of instruments. It includes the modern, side-blown or transverse flute, recorders, fifes and whistles. All of these are woodwind instruments, like the clarinet, oboe and bassoon. In ancient times, flutes were used in sacred ceremonies to evoke spirits, and were sacred to the Hindu God Krishna.

The beautiful, pure sound of the flute is heard above the other instruments of the orchestra. The flute is a hollow tube, stopped at one end. Near the stopped end is a mouthpiece. The musician blows across the mouthpiece to cause the air inside the instrument to vibrate and produce sound. Other holes are bored along the body, to produce a range of notes.

Padded keys are suspended over the holes, on rods that are soldered on to the tube. Each metal key has a soft pad inside it. When you press down the key with your finger, the pad forms an air-tight seal over the hole beneath, to alter the pitch of the note. A spring returns the key to its original position once you release it.

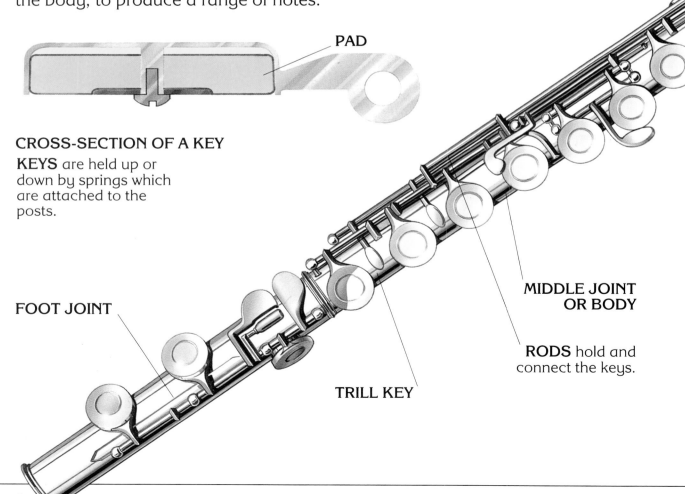

PAD

CROSS-SECTION OF A KEY

KEYS are held up or down by springs which are attached to the posts.

FOOT JOINT

TRILL KEY

MIDDLE JOINT OR BODY

RODS hold and connect the keys.

Young Musician

Playing the

Flute

Recorder

788.3

d

New edition published in 2003
© Aladdin Books 2003

Designed and produced by
Aladdin Books Ltd
28 Percy Street
London W1T 2BZ

First published in
Great Britain in 1993 by
Franklin Watts
96 Leonard Street
London EC2A 4XD

ISBN: 0 7496 5120 2

Printed in UAE

A CIP record for this book is available
from the British Library.

The author, Simon Walton, teaches
the flute at all levels and maintains a
freelance performing career spanning
recital, concerto, contemporary and
orchestral works.

The author thanks Andy, Jon and
Patrick at Top Wind, London, and
Nigel and Duncan at All Flutes Plus,
London.

The consultant, Michael Short, is a
composer and part-time professor of
music history at the Royal Military
School of Music, Knellar Hall.

Music copyright © Simon Walton
1992 unless otherwise stated

Series designer: David West
Design: Peter Bennett
Editor: Jen Green
Picture researcher: Emma Krikler
Illustrators: Ron Hayward,
                     David West,
                     David Russell

CONTENTS

INTRODUCTION	4
GETTING TO KNOW YOUR FLUTE	6
MAKING A START	8
FIRST NOTES	10
ADDING THE BEAT	12
MOVING ON	14
THE SECOND OCTAVE	16
FIRST MELODIES	18
REACHING THE THIRD OCTAVE	20
PLAYING TOGETHER	22
FLUTE FINGERING CHART	24
PLAYING THE RECORDER	26
THE WORLD OF WOODWIND	28
COMPOSERS AND PERFORMERS	30
GLOSSARY	31
INDEX	32

Not all of the keys are pressed down with your fingers. Others are linked with rods to those you do press down.

EMBOUCHURE OR BLOW HOLE

LIP PLATE

RIB

SPRING

POST

HEAD JOINT

CROWN

CORK

The end of the flute is plugged with a cork squeezed between two metal discs. These are held on a threaded post which moves up and down the tube as you twist the crown.

Flutes and recorders are called woodwind instruments because they were originally made of wood. Nowadays most flutes are made of metal, although wood is still used for the recorder and the piccolo.

In the 19th century, some show flutes were made of glass. Ivory, porcelain and carbon fibre have also been used. Cork, felt, cardboard, and even the lining from cows' abdomens are used in the manufacture of the pads.

Professional flutes are often made of solid silver. Student flutes are often made with a nickel-silver alloy, which actually contains no silver but is a kind of white brass, plated with silver. Flutes can also be made of gold.

GETTING TO KNOW YOUR FLUTE

Your flute is made in three parts. Take care when putting it together, as it is quite easy to damage. Hold the parts of the flute where there are no keys, and go slowly and carefully at first.

Ease the middle and foot joints together first, twisting them to and fro. Line up the rod on the foot with the keys on the body.

Twist and slide the head into the body next. Line up the middle of the blow hole with the centres of most of the keys.

Now take up your flute and position your fingers above the keys as shown below and on page 9. Your left thumb is held against its key at an angle. Your flute is supported at the base of the first finger of your left hand, and by your right hand thumb, which goes behind, not underneath, the flute. These two contact points, with your chin, keep the flute supported and balanced. Your other fingers are free to work the keys.

It is important to be relaxed and comfortable when playing the flute. Get ready to play by holding your flute pointing out in front of you, with the head joint above your left shoulder. Swivel the flute around to the right, until your shoulders are stretched. Turn your head to the left and bring your flute up to your mouth. You should be looking over your elbow, as shown above.

Stand up straight with your feet a shoulder-width apart. Don't lock your knees.

CARING FOR YOUR FLUTE

Protect your flute from sudden changes in temperature. Never leave it near a radiator; metal may warp, and wooden piccolos can crack. Warm up your flute simply by playing or by holding it in your hands. Blowing harshly through the flute may warm it too quickly. Clean your flute after you have finished playing. Moisture will rot the pads, and can swell and crack wooden instruments. Thread a cotton cloth through your cleaning stick. Clean each joint separately. Push the stick into the head gently. Don't allow the stick to scratch the inside. Dust the outside with a clean paintbrush. Don't adjust keys, springs or screws unless you are quite sure of what you are doing. Ask your teacher to help instead.

MAKING A START

Your first sounds on the flute are made by blowing into the head only. Place the lip plate under your bottom lip, so you feel the edge of the hole against the edge of your lip. Make an "oo" shape with your mouth, and blow across the hole as if you are blowing a bubble.

Cover the open end of the head joint with the palm of your hand at first. Keep the sides of your mouth relaxed and your breath even.

Now take your hand off the end. Practise long notes, keeping the sound steady. It may take a while to produce a good sound.

The shape that you make with your lips is called an embouchure (pronounced om-boo-sure). Use a mirror to check that yours is in the centre of your mouth. Direct your breath towards the opposite rim of the blow hole.

When you blow across the hole, some air passes into the flute, and some passes over it. This causes the air inside the flute to vibrate. Try rolling the flute in and out to cover less and more of the hole.

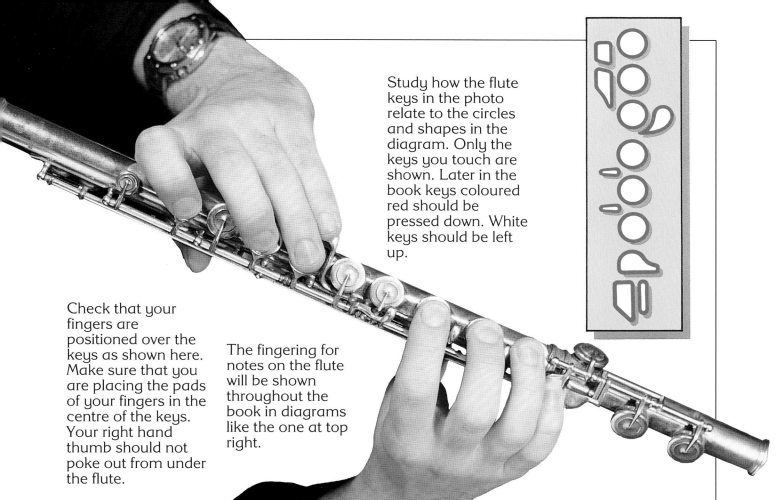

Study how the flute keys in the photo relate to the circles and shapes in the diagram. Only the keys you touch are shown. Later in the book keys coloured red should be pressed down. White keys should be left up.

Check that your fingers are positioned over the keys as shown here. Make sure that you are placing the pads of your fingers in the centre of the keys. Your right hand thumb should not poke out from under the flute.

The fingering for notes on the flute will be shown throughout the book in diagrams like the one at top right.

EARLY FLUTES

The flute family is very ancient. The earliest flutes which have survived are thought to be 20,000 years old. They were sometimes used in religious rites. Early flutes were made of many different natural materials, such as bone, stone, wood, horn and shell. Historians believe that flutes originated in central Asia. They were carried by traders along silk trading routes, to reach China around 5000 BC. The Chinese flute, the *Tse*, has remained virtually unchanged since then. The flute reached India and Mediterranean lands as late as 200 BC. Flutes have been played by shepherds tending their flocks for thousands of years. Different kinds of flutes are found in many parts of the world, including Tibet, below.

FIRST NOTES

Written music can look daunting, but it's really quite simple. Musical notes are named after the letters of the alphabet, from A to G. After G the letters begin again. Notes appear on a set of five lines, called a stave. The position of notes on the stave tells you how high or low they sound.

B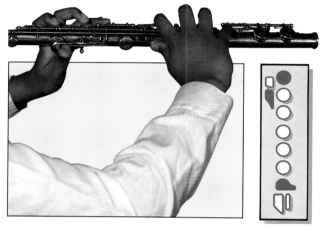

The note B appears on the middle line of the stave. Press down the thumb and first finger of the left hand, and the right hand little finger.

A

The note A is a tone below B, and is written in the space below the line for B. Press down either thumb key, although the one on the right is best.

G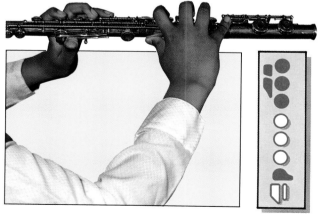

The note G is a tone below A and sits on the line below it. Notice that the notes become lower the more keys you press down.

Now try the tunes below, using B, A and G. The next page deals with notes of different lengths. Make all the notes the same length here, and play them steadily and evenly. As you play, remember to stand straight, with relaxed shoulders and knees. Keep your head up. Music can be used to create all sorts of moods. The mood may be indicated at the beginning of the music, as it is in the third piece below.

The treble clef at the start of the music indicates the pitch of notes. Breathe deeply and blow the air out steadily as you play.

Listen to your sound. Are you making the best noise you can? Practise these pieces until you can play them through confidently.

Slow and sad

BAROQUE FLUTES

One of the first European side-blown flutes was the *Schwegal*, played by German soldiers in the 12th century. By the Baroque period (from around 1600 to 1750) flutes were cone-shaped, wider at the head end, and tapering off at the foot. Johann Joachim Quantz (1697-1773), right, was an important flute player and teacher. He was court composer to Frederick the Great of Prussia, and taught Frederick the flute.

ADDING THE BEAT

The beat, or pulse, is vital to a piece of music. It is what sets your foot tapping or your fingers drumming to the tune. In written music, long and short notes are represented by different symbols. The beat remains constant, at whatever speed you have decided to play. The rhythm, or pattern of long and short notes, varies within the basic beat.

One whole-note or semibreve =

Two half-notes or minims =

Four quarter-notes or crotchets =

Eight eighth-notes or quavers.

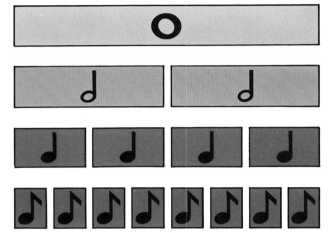

Symbols for the notes of different time values are shown above. Reading from the top down, each note is twice the time value of the one below it.

Memorise the symbols, and try counting or clapping each line. Most pieces are counted in quarter-notes (crotchets), so count four for a semibreve and two for a minim.

RESTS

Silence can be as important as sound in music. In written music, silence is shown by symbols called rests. A rest often makes the audience more alert, waiting to hear what is coming next. Rests of different time values correspond to all the notes you have met. Think of rests as silent notes, and count them just as carefully as played notes.

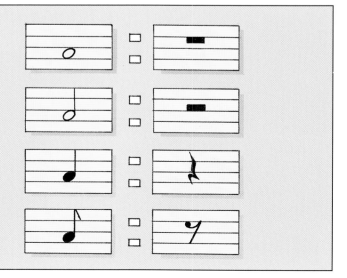

Written music is divided into bars. Pieces of music have different numbers of beats in the bar. This is shown by the time signature after the treble clef. The bottom figure tells you what note indicates the beat, and the top figure tells you how many there are in a bar. So 3/4 time has three crotchets in a bar, and so on. Try clapping or counting the pieces before you play them. A dot after a note increases its time value by half.

At walking speed

Briskly as if running

Dancing

CHARLES NICHOLSON

Baroque flutes had six or seven holes. In the 18th century, holes were added to produce clearer notes. Keys were introduced to cover the holes that the flutist's fingers could not reach easily. Flutes were still conical.

Charles Nicholson (1795-1837), right, was an English flute-player renowned for his full sound and brilliant technique. He lived in London, where flutes became very popular in the 19th century. Flute clubs appeared all over the city, and learning the instrument was seen as part of the schooling of an English gentleman.

MOVING ON

Over the next two pages there are six new notes, which will help you play more tunes. Changing notes between C and D will really test how well you have your flute in balance, as every finger has to change except for the little finger of the left hand. Make sure your flute is not rolling back when you play.

C can be difficult to balance, as you have only your left hand first finger and right hand little finger down. Keep your right thumb against the flute, and make sure it doesn't roll back.

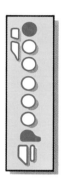

If you have difficulty playing the low notes, make sure that you are keeping your head up. It is tempting to move your head up and down as you try to play high and low.

E is your lowest note yet. You may have to press the keys more firmly for the low notes, as old flute pads may leak. Try not to make this a habit. It will shorten the life of the pads.

Practise the new notes on their own first, then try the exercises below. Look at the time signatures, and clap the rhythms before you play. The signs linking the notes in the first piece are slurs (see page 15).

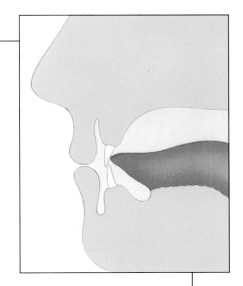

SHARPS AND FLATS

Sharps and flats, the black notes on a piano, fit between the "natural" notes, the white notes on a piano. B flat is half a tone lower than B – try them both and listen to the difference. F sharp is half a tone higher than F. Fingerings for these notes are given here. The piece below includes them.

TONGUING

So far you have blown evenly to produce a continuous noise. The technique of tonguing breaks up the stream of sound, to begin notes more cleanly. Tonguing makes little sound, but neatens the start of the note.

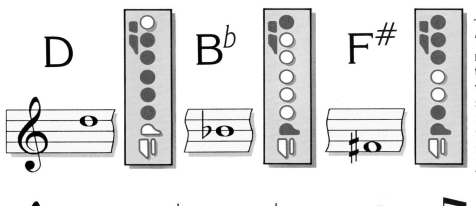

D B♭ F♯

Tongue by saying "te" as you blow a note, quickly touching your teeth with your tongue, as shown above. When reading music, tongue each note, unless notes are joined with a slur.

DESIGNER OF THE MODERN FLUTE

Theobald Boehm (1794-1881) was a German flutist and goldsmith. He was responsible for the creation of the modern flute. Inspired by the sound of Charles Nicholson, Boehm decided to make a flute which would produce loud, clear notes. He designed an instrument with all the holes needed to produce the notes in the octave (see page 16). He invented the system of keys still used today, with a few minor changes. Boehm's early models were still cone-shaped, but later versions had a cylindrical body and conical head.

THE SECOND OCTAVE

You can play a sequence of seven natural notes, going up from E to D. After D the sequence begins again with E. This is an octave. The higher E is played with the same fingering as the E you know. Make your embouchure smaller, and speed up your air stream. Move your jaw forward and direct your air stream a little higher.

All the notes from E to C in the second octave are produced in the same way. Practise them, using the fingerings you know. The first picture shows the shape of the air column inside your flute for the notes in the first octave. The air vibrates twice as fast when you play notes in the

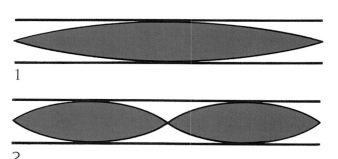

second octave. The other diagrams show how the air column vibrates as even higher notes are played. Learn to recognise the sound of an octave by practising the first piece below. High notes appear above the stave. You will notice that extra lines, called ledger lines, reach up to the notes.

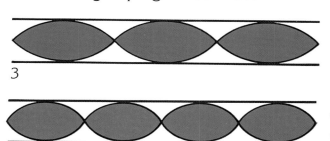

Slowly and carefully

Evenly

Briskly

GOOD AND BAD HABITS

Bad habits are easy to develop, and hard to stop once they become familiar! Bad posture can cause a lot of pain when you are older. Remember to stand up straight and keep your breathing deep and even. This will allow you to play more notes without gasping for breath, or feeling faint from lack of oxygen!

Listen to yourself as you are playing, and try to improve your tone. Practise regularly, every day if possible. Try to practise at the same time each day, or you may never get around to it!

Our flutist has developed some very bad habits. How many can you spot?

BUYING YOUR OWN FLUTE

If you decide to buy your own flute, ask your teacher for advice. If possible, go to a specialist flute shop, where you will find a good choice of instruments. The shop should check each flute thoroughly before putting it on sale.

Take a piece of music you know to the shop so that you can try out various flutes. Try a few of the same model if you can, as they can vary. If possible, arrange to take the flute away with you for a trial period, so you and your teacher can test it.

Hold your head and your flute up, but keep your shoulders down and relaxed. Don't cross your legs when you play! Keep your feet a shoulder-width apart. When reading music, stand at a sensible distance from the music stand, otherwise you may start lowering your head to read.

FIRST MELODIES

Now you are ready to try some melodies. Below are well-known pieces by Mozart and Verdi. Practising a tune you know will leave you free to concentrate on your sound. You may also be able to listen to the same melodies performed by famous musicians.

PRACTICE AND PERFORMANCE
Use a mirror when you are practising, to check your posture, hands and embouchure. In an examination or concert, try to relax, and remember to breathe deeply. Make yourself comfortable: adjust your music stand to suit your height, and make sure you can see both your pianist and audience.

THEME FROM CLARINET QUINTET **MOZART ARR. WALTON**

Study the music carefully. This piece is in 4/4 time, with four crotchets to the bar. Clap the rhythm. A dot above or under a note indicates that it should be played *staccato*, as a short note. Don't rush staccato notes, and don't end a note with your tongue.

Dotted notes are worth one and a half times their usual value. The notes with double tails are semiquavers, worth half the time value of a quaver. The dotted quaver and semiquaver together make up one crotchet beat.

A metronome (left) will help you keep to the beat when you are practising. If you find you can't keep up, set the metronome on a slower speed.

LA DONNA È MOBILE
VERDI ARR. WALTON

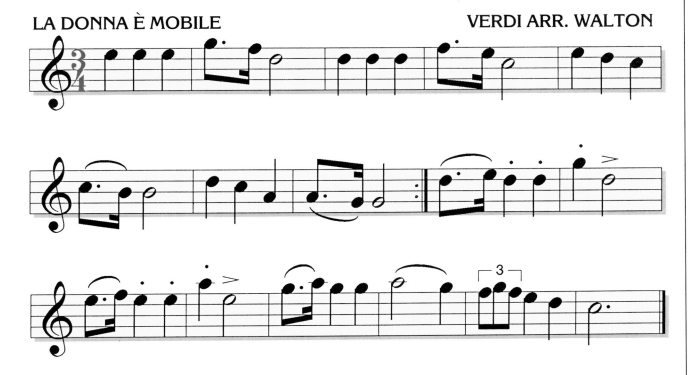

The double bar line with two dots in the middle line is a repeat sign. Return to the start and play the music again, before going on. The symbols like hairpins are accents. Blow these notes more strongly. Near the end is a triplet of three quavers, played in the time usually taken for two.

MARCEL MOYSE

Marcel Moyse (1889-1984), right, was a brilliant flutist and great character. He influenced the French flute school, which became famous for warm and expressive playing. In the 1930s, Moyse had a demanding schedule as a concert artist and teacher. He often travelled overnight between Paris, Geneva and other European cities on his beloved motorcycle. Geoffrey Gilbert (1914-1989) introduced the French style of playing to Britain. Gilbert was an important 20th century British flutist.

REACHING THE THIRD OCTAVE

The sound you make on the flute depends on your control over the air you blow out. Practise regulating your breathing. Lie on the floor with your hands on your stomach, just under your rib cage. Breathe in and out slowly and deeply. As you expand your rib cage, air is drawn into your lungs. Your hands should rise with your stomach.

THE THIRD OCTAVE

The fingerings in the third octave are more complicated. To sound the notes, you need to tighten your embouchure and speed up your air jet, as you did for the second octave. Notes may sound squeaky at first, but will improve with practice.

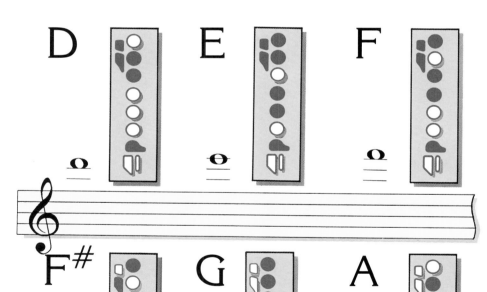

Practise the changes of fingering between these notes. Don't practise the flute only in the third octave; your lower octaves will suffer and so will your neighbours!

Now practise the notes D to A in all three octaves, playing loudly and softly. Memorise these new fingerings and try to hit each note cleanly as you move up the octaves.

The exercise below will help you to practise finger changes. It is in 4/4 time. As you change notes, move all your fingers together, quickly and smoothly, like a robot. Slur the notes as written, and listen out for slips as you change fingering. Notice the natural signs in bars eight and nine. They tell you to play F natural, not F sharp.

Evenly

MAKING A FLUTE

A flute is a hollow tube with holes for mouth and fingers. Make your own from bamboo, plastic or rubber tube. Stop one end with a bottle cork, or even plasticine. Make a blow hole between five and 20 millimetres from the stopper. You may need an adult to help with this. Now make holes for your fingers.

Position the holes as you choose, or take measurements from a penny whistle or six-hole flute.

PLAYING TOGETHER

Playing with others can be fun. Below are two pieces for you to play with friends or with your teacher. Neither has the parts written out one below the other, as you would expect. The first is a canon. One player begins, and the second starts when the first reaches the note marked 2*. Other players can begin as the first reaches 3*, 4*, and so on.

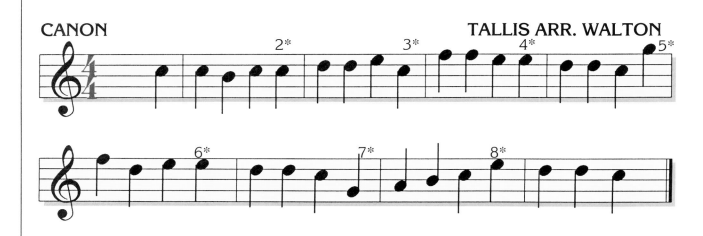

CANON   TALLIS ARR. WALTON

Good posture will help your sound. When you are sight-reading, try not to lean forward towards the music. Your head will come down and disturb your embouchure. When sharing a music stand, arrange your flutes so that you and your partner don't bump into each other. It may be easier if the player on the left puts his or her flute behind the other player. Don't swing round with your flute up! This piece is in 4/4 time and begins on the fourth beat of the bar. Count yourself in aloud, and try to keep to an even tempo (speed) throughout.

A duet is a piece of music for two players. This one is special, and should be placed flat between two players. Both start at the same time and read the music from opposite sides. Again, count yourselves in and keep an even beat. Try to reach the end at the same time!

UPSIDE-DOWN MINUET

DOPPLER EFFECT

During the 18th and 19th centuries, *virtuouso* or very skilled performers would tour the cities of Europe giving concerts. The Doppler brothers, Carl and Franz, were a famous duo of flutists who toured in the middle of the 19th century. To prevent the possibility of tangling flutes and so that audiences could see the flying fingers of both players, Carl Doppler had a special flute built that he could play to the left.

FLUTE FINGERING CHART

Below is a fingering chart complete up to top F$^{\#}$. Where two fingerings are given for one note, the alternative will sometimes produce a better sound. Try them all.

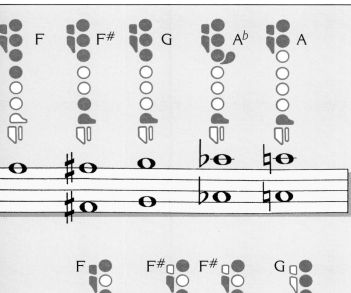

F F# G A♭ A

F F# F# G

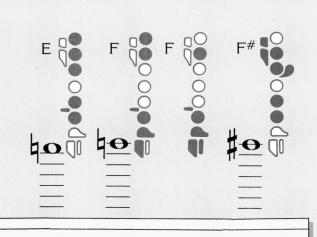

E F F F#

SPECIAL EFFECTS

Professional flutists use a variety of techniques to widen the range of notes they can produce.

VIBRATO

Vibrato is a technique which imitates the voices of opera singers. Try it once you can produce an even, pure sound. Without tonguing, make accented notes to a steady tone, as if you were saying "Ha-Ha-Ha". Speed them up gradually, to form a vibrato.

fast passages, professional flutists use double or triple tonguing. Try it out for yourself. Practise saying "Te-ke" for double and "Te-ke-te" for triple tonguing.

MULTI-PHONICS

Multiphonics involves playing more than one note at once on the flute. Instead of moving cleanly up to the next octave, widen your air stream to cover both notes until they sound together.

Other modern techniques include note-bending and key-tapping. For note-bending, move your jaw in or out to cover more or less of the hole with your top lip. This makes the note bend higher or lower. Key-tapping involves fingering loudly while not always blowing, so that the noise of the keys can be heard.

FLUTTER TONGUING

Flutter tonguing is popular in modern music. It is done by rolling a long "rrrrr" with your tongue, or by gargling in the back of the throat while blowing!

DOUBLE AND TRIPLE TONGUING

When tonguing very

PLAYING THE RECORDER

The recorder is a member of the flute family. At various times in history it has been more popular than the flute. Recorders are made of wood or plastic, and can be quite cheap to buy. The simplicity of the recorder makes it a good instrument for beginners, who may later change to the flute or another member of the woodwind family.

Blowing into a slot in the mouthpiece directs a stream of air against the edge of an opening called the fipple. Air flows alternately over and into the recorder, to set the air vibrating inside the instrument.

Notice how the fingerholes on the recorder correspond to the diagram below. The extra key in the diagram top right is for the left hand thumb, which fits underneath the recorder.

HEAD

MOUTHPIECE

FIPPLE

BODY

FINGERHOLES

FOOT

MICHALA PETRI

Michala Petri is one of the most famous recorder players today. She was born in Denmark, and made her first professional appearance at the age of eight. Michala Petri plays music from both the baroque and contemporary periods. She gives concerts all over the world, helping to restore the popularity of the recorder.

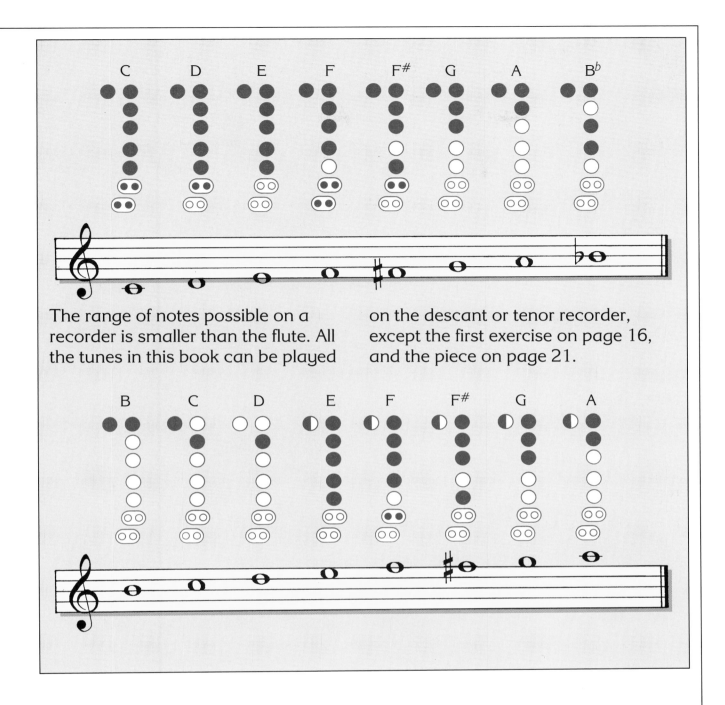

The range of notes possible on a recorder is smaller than the flute. All the tunes in this book can be played on the descant or tenor recorder, except the first exercise on page 16, and the piece on page 21.

The recorder was a popular instrument in the late middle ages, and has remained virtually unchanged since then. Music from the baroque period now played on the flute was written for the recorder. Recently, recorders have become more popular again. There has been a great interest in hearing music from previous centuries played on the instruments for which it was written.

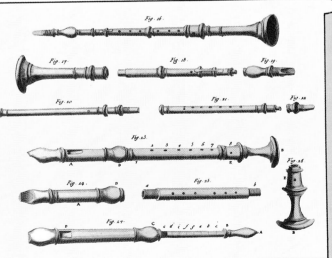

THE WORLD OF WOODWIND

The woodwind family includes the clarinet, oboe, bassoon and saxophone, which use a single or double reed to make the air vibrate inside the instrument. Many different kinds of musicians play woodwind instruments, from the busker on the street corner to the folk or jazz player, and the professional in the concert hall.

Woodwind instruments are important in the orchestra, and are also used in chamber music, played by a small group of musicians. The wind quintet (see page 29) is a popular combination for chamber music, but almost any group of instruments can play. The position of woodwind in the orchestra is shown below right.

Flutes and other woodwind instruments are used as solo concert instruments, or are accompanied by the piano, harp or guitar. Baroque music now performed by the flute and piano was probably written for another keyboard instrument, the harpsichord. A good performer will communicate with both the accompanist and the audience.

If you get the chance, join a chamber group or an orchestra. Look out for these orchestral pieces with famous woodwind passages:
Debussy, *L'Après-midi d'un Faune*
Stravinsky, *Petrouchka* and *Firebird*
Saint-Saëns, *Carnival of the Animals*
Prokofiev, *Peter and the Wolf*
Rossini, *William Tell Overture*

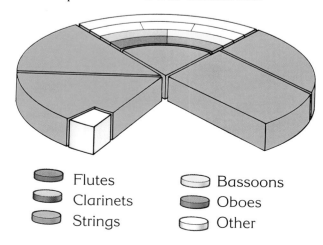

Flutes Bassoons
Clarinets Oboes
Strings Other

JAMES GALWAY

James Galway is one of the best known flutists performing today. He is famous for his golden flute and the recordings he has made of concertos by Khachaturian and Rodrigo – the second of these was actually written for Galway. These pieces show off his bright, brilliant sound, and his superb tongue and finger technique.

Flute   Oboe   Horn   Clarinet   Bassoon

The standard woodwind instruments are the flute, clarinet, oboe and bassoon. Each instrument has larger or smaller relatives which produce a lower or higher sound. The little cousin of the flute is the piccolo, which is pitched an octave higher.

The clarinet, oboe and bassoon all have vibrating reeds. The oboe has a double reed and a conical shape, opening out at the bottom. It produces a mellow sound. Richard Strauss and Vaughan Williams have written concertos for the oboe.

The clarinet has a single reed which vibrates against the mouthpiece. It has a beautiful, liquid sound and a range of three and a half octaves. Clarinets emerged in the 18th century, and were improved by Boehm. The bass clarinet is pitched an octave lower.

The bassoon has a distinct tone, which can sound comic or sorrowful. It, too, has a double reed. Its relative, the contrabassoon, plays an octave lower. The wind quintet (above) is completed by the horn, a member of the family of brass instruments.

COMPOSERS AND PERFORMERS

In mediaeval times, the recorder was the most widely played woodwind instrument. Music began to be written for the flute in the 17th century, and it has been an instrument popular with composers since that time. The flute and other woodwind instruments are used in jazz, folk and rock as well as in classical music.

Frederick the Great

Antonio Vivaldi (1675-1741) was known as the "red priest " because of his red hair. His most famous work is *The Four Seasons*, a set of four violin concertos, but he also wrote many concertos and sonatas for the flute.
Georg Telemann (1681-1767) was a prolific German composer, who wrote 12 solo fantasias and many sonatas.
Georg Frideric Handel (1685-1759) was born in Germany but moved to England. He heard a concert by Quantz and later

wrote 11 sonatas for flute and recorder.
Johann Sebastian Bach (1685-1750) is probably the most famous composer of the Baroque period. He was also a choirmaster and a brilliant organist. One of his last

W A Mozart

works, *The Musical Offering*, was written for Frederick the Great. His many works for the flute include the B minor suite.
Johann Joachim Quantz (1697-1773) was court composer to **Frederick the**

Great of Prussia (1712-86). Quantz composed more than 300 flute concertos, and Frederick himself also wrote music for the flute. Inspired by Quantz, the composers Vivaldi and Handel began to write more music

Friedrich Kuhlau

for the flute.
Christoph Willibald Gluck (1714-1787) is loved by flutists for his beautiful "Dance of the Blessed Spirits " from his opera *Orfeo ed Euridice* (1762).
Wolfgang Amadeus Mozart

(1756-1791) was a child prodigy, who gave concerts all over Europe from the age of five. His flute quartets and concertos are very popular. His last opera was *The Magic Flute*. Its hero, Tamino, is protected on his quest by the flute given him by the Queen of the Night.
Daniel Friedrich Kuhlau (1786-1832) and **Theobald Boehm** (1794-1881) were brilliant flute players during a time when the flute was extremely popular. Many of the pieces they wrote are light

Sergei Prokofiev

but technically demanding.

During the Romantic period **Carl Reinecke** (1824-1910) wrote full-blooded music for the flute. The concertino by **Cecille Chaminade** (1857-1944) has a delightful Hollywood-style opening and furious technical sections.

Claude Debussy (1862-1918) was a French pianist-composer. His *L'Après-midi d'un Faune* begins with a haunting flute solo, and his *Syrinx* is possibly the best known solo piece for the instrument.

Carl Nielson (1865-1931) and

Pierre Boulez

Jacques Ibert (1890-1959) wrote two of the best-known 20th-century concertos for the flute.

Sergei Prokofiev (1891-1953) was another child prodigy, who wrote his first opera when he was nine years

old. His work *Peter and the Wolf* provides a delightful guide to the instruments in the orchestra.

Bohuslav Martinu (1890-1959), **Paul Hindemith** (1895-1963) and **Francis Poulenc** (1899-1963) also wrote

Paul Edmund Davies

wonderful sonatas for the flute.

Pierre Boulez (1925-) is a French composer and conductor whose sonatine contains modern techniques, giving the flute a wide range of expression.

Outstanding contemporary flute players include **Jean-Pierre Rampal** from France, **Paul Edmund Davies**, **William Bennett** and **Susan Milan** from Britain, **Julius Baker** from America, **Paul Meisen** from Germany and **Peter-Lukas Graf** from Switzerland.

GLOSSARY

Chamber music music for small groups of players. It takes its name from the fact that it was once played in the chambers (rooms) in private houses.

Conical shaped like a cone.

Concerto a work for a solo instrument accompanied by an orchestra.

Cylindrical shaped like a roller.

Embouchure shaping of the lips to the mouthpiece of an instrument.

Flat lowers a note by half a tone.

Ledger lines lines that can be added to the musical stave for notes too high or low to fit within the stave.

Mechanism the moving parts of an instrument, such as the keys on the flute.

Metronome machine that sounds regular beats at a speed that can be adjusted. The figures on the metronome indicate the number of beats per minute.

Natural note that is not sharpened or flattened.

Octave interval between eight natural notes. Two notes an octave apart have the same letter name.

Sharp raises a note by half a tone.

Sonata a work for piano, or for a solo instrument and piano.

Stave group of five lines on which musical notes are written.

Technique method of playing, or skilful performance.

Treble clef indicates the pitch of the notes in written music.

INDEX

Bach, Johann Sebastian 30
baroque music 27, 28
bars 13
bassoon 4, 28, 29
beat 12, 13, 19
Boehm, Theobald 15, 29, 30-1
Boulez, Pierre 31
breathing 17, 20
buying a flute 17

canon 22
caring for your flute 7
ceremonial use 4, 9
chamber music 28, 31
Chaminade, Cecille 31
Chinese flute 9
clarinet 4, 28, 29
cleaning your flute 7
composers 30-1
concertos 29, 30, 31
concerts 18
contrabassoon 29
control 20
cork 5
crotchets 12

Debussy, Claude 28, 31
Doppler brothers 23
dotted notes 13, 18
double and triple

tonguing 25
duets 23

embouchure 5, 8, 16, 20, 22, 31
examinations 18

fifes 4
fingering 9, 20, 21
fingering chart 24-5
fipple 26
flats 15, 31
flute parts 4-5
flutter tonguing 25
foot joint 4, 6

Galway, James 29
Gilbert, Geoffrey 19
Gluck, Christoph Willibald 30

Handel, Georg Frideric 30
head joint 5
horn 29

Ibert, Jacques 31

key-tapping 25
keys 4, 5, 9, 13
Kuhlau, Daniel Friedrich 30-1

ledger lines 16, 31
lip plate 5
making a flute 21
metronome 19, 31
middle joint 4, 6

minims 12
mouthpiece 4
Moyse, Marcel 19
Mozart, Wolfgang Amadeus 30
multiphonics 25

naturals 15, 31
Nicholson, Charles 13
Nielson, Carl 31
note-bending 25
notes 4, 10-11, 12, 13, 14-16, 20

oboe 4, 28, 29
octaves 16, 20, 31
orchestral pieces 28

pads 4, 5, 7
performers 30-1
Petri, Michala 26
piccolo 5, 29
pitch 11
playing together 22-3
posture 7, 11, 17, 22
practising 17, 18, 20
Prokofiev, Sergei 28, 31

Quantz, Johann Joachim 11, 30
recorder 4, 5, 26-7, 30
reeds 28, 29

Reinecke, Carl 31
relaxed position 7, 11, 17
rests 12
rhythm 12
rods 4, 5

saxophone 28
Schwegal 11
semibreves 12
semiquavers 18
sharps 15, 31
sonatas 30, 31
staccato notes 18
starting to play 8-9
stave 10, 31
symphony orchestra 28

technique 25, 31
Telemann, Georg 30
tempo 22
time signature 13
tonguing 15, 25
treble clef 11, 31
trill keys 4

vibrato 25
Vivaldi, Antonio 3

whistles 4
wind quintet 28, 29
woodwind instruments 4, 5, 28, 29, 30
written music 10, 12, 13, 18, 19

Photocredits

Abbreviations: l-left, r-right, b-bottom, t-top, c-centre, m-middle, Front cover — Flick Smith. 5, 6 all, 7 both, 8 all, 9t, 9m, 10 all, 11l, 14, 17 both, 18, 21 all, 22, 23t, 25, 28b, 29m — Roger Vlitos. 9b, 29t — Frank Spooner Pictures. 11r, 15, 30ml — Mary Evans Picture Library. 13, 19, 23b, 30mr — Royal College of Music. 26 — BMG Classics. 27, 30t, 30b — Hulton Deutsch. 28t — Robert Harding Picture Library. 31t — Michael Owen. 31 — British Broadcasting Company.